# EARTH CYCLES

# EARTH CYCLES

MICHAEL ELSOHN ROSS

ILLUSTRATED BY GUSTAV MOORE

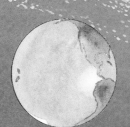

**M** MILLBROOK PRESS • MINNEAPOLIS

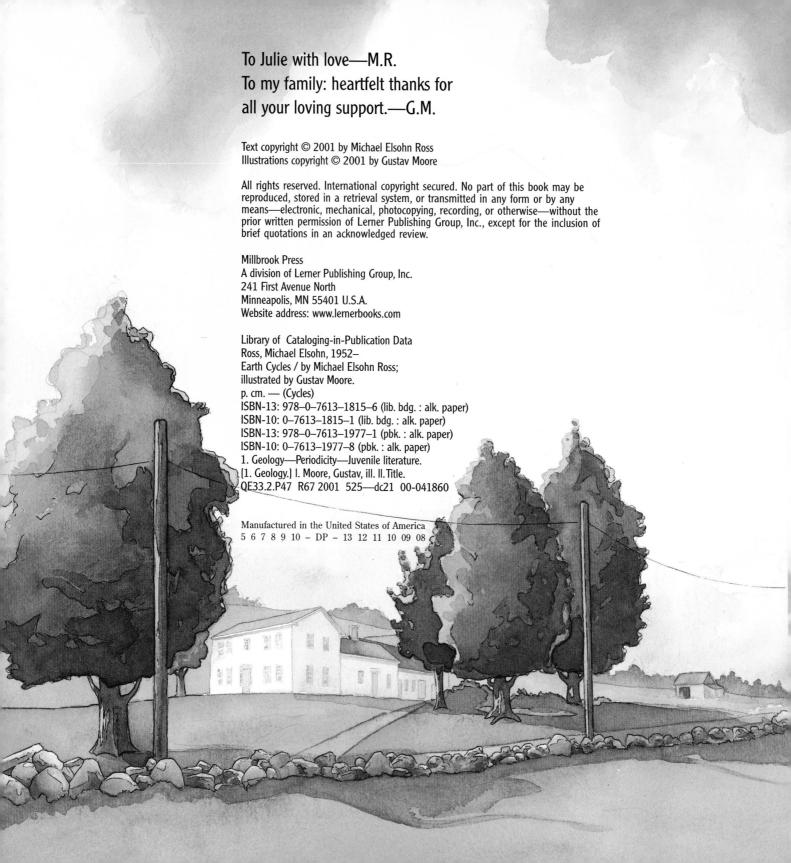

To Julie with love—M.R.
To my family: heartfelt thanks for
all your loving support.—G.M.

Text copyright © 2001 by Michael Elsohn Ross
Illustrations copyright © 2001 by Gustav Moore

Millbrook Press
A division of Lerner Publishing Group, Inc.
241 First Avenue North
Minneapolis, MN 55401 U.S.A.
Website address: www.lernerbooks.com

Library of Cataloging-in-Publication Data
Ross, Michael Elsohn, 1952–
Earth Cycles / by Michael Elsohn Ross;
illustrated by Gustav Moore.
p. cm. — (Cycles)
ISBN-13: 978–0–7613–1815–6 (lib. bdg. : alk. paper)
ISBN-10: 0–7613–1815–1 (lib. bdg. : alk. paper)
ISBN-13: 978–0–7613–1977–1 (pbk. : alk. paper)
ISBN-10: 0–7613–1977–8 (pbk. : alk. paper)
1. Geology—Periodicity—Juvenile literature.
[1. Geology.] I. Moore, Gustav, ill. II. Title.
QE33.2.P47 R67 2001 525—dc21 00-041860

Manufactured in the United States of America
5 6 7 8 9 10 – DP – 13 12 11 10 09 08

The Earth is round like a ball
and it moves in circular motions.
It changes in patterns that go round and round
like the wheels on a bike.
Events that repeat over and over again in the same
way are called cycles.

# DAY CYCLES

The Earth spins all the time.
It goes round and round like a very slow top.
It takes a whole day to make one spin.

As it spins, each part of the Earth takes a turn facing the Sun and being bathed in light.
The part of the Earth that faces the Sun has daytime.

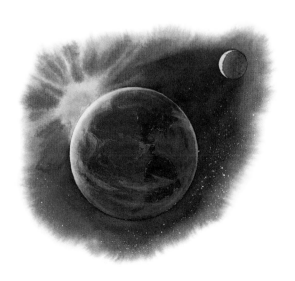

As it spins, each part of the Earth takes a turn facing away from the Sun and is covered in darkness.
The part that faces away from the Sun has nighttime.

Each day, you ride on a slowly spinning planet Earth
from day to night and back.
Each day you move through light to dark
and back again.
You ride the day cycle.

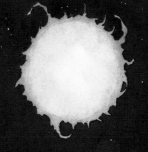

# DAY FACTS

A day is
24 hours.

WINTER

SPRING

SUMMER

FALL

Daylight length varies from season to season on each part of the Earth.

Each day, as the Earth spins toward the Sun's light, we see the Sun first appear in the east and at the end of the day disappear in the west.

# MOON AROUND

The Moon travels in a circle, too.
Never stopping, always changing,
it circles around the Earth.

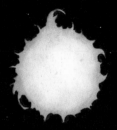

The Moon is like a mirror reflecting sunlight.
From where we watch on Earth, the Moon appears
to change shape from night to night.
What we see is the Moon reflecting more light or less light.

This Moon mirror changes from a sliver
to a sideways grin.
It changes from a half circle
to a giant disk.

Then it finally begins
to slowly fade, night by night,
into darkness
before appearing again.
Once more it is a sliver in the night sky that is
ready to go on another moon cycle … a circle of moons.

# MOON FACTS

The moon cycle takes a little less than 27 days.

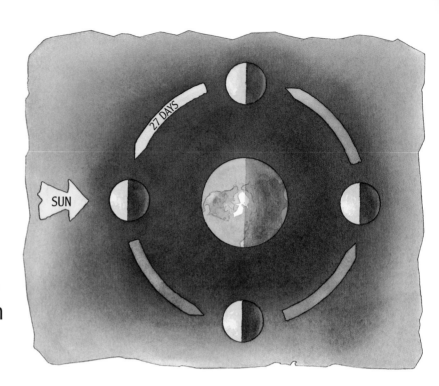

There are 13 lunar cycles in a year.

The tides are higher and lower during full moons.

# THE CYCLE OF SEASONS

Some spaceships have pointed prows and fins.
Ours is a sphere, like a giant orange.
It is called the Earth and you travel on it around the Sun.
Each journey takes a whole year.

Each orbit around the Sun
is a trip through the seasons.
You travel from chilly winters . . .

to mild springs . . .

into hot summers
and on to cool autumns.
At the end of autumn is a new winter
and then another year…
the beginning of another cycle of seasons.

March

# YEAR FACTS

SUMMER SOLSTICE IN THE NORTH

A year is 365 days.

Each season is 3 months long.

The shortest day of the year is called the winter solstice.

The longest day is called the summer solstice.

JANUARY

FEBRUARY

MARCH

APRIL

MAY

JUNE

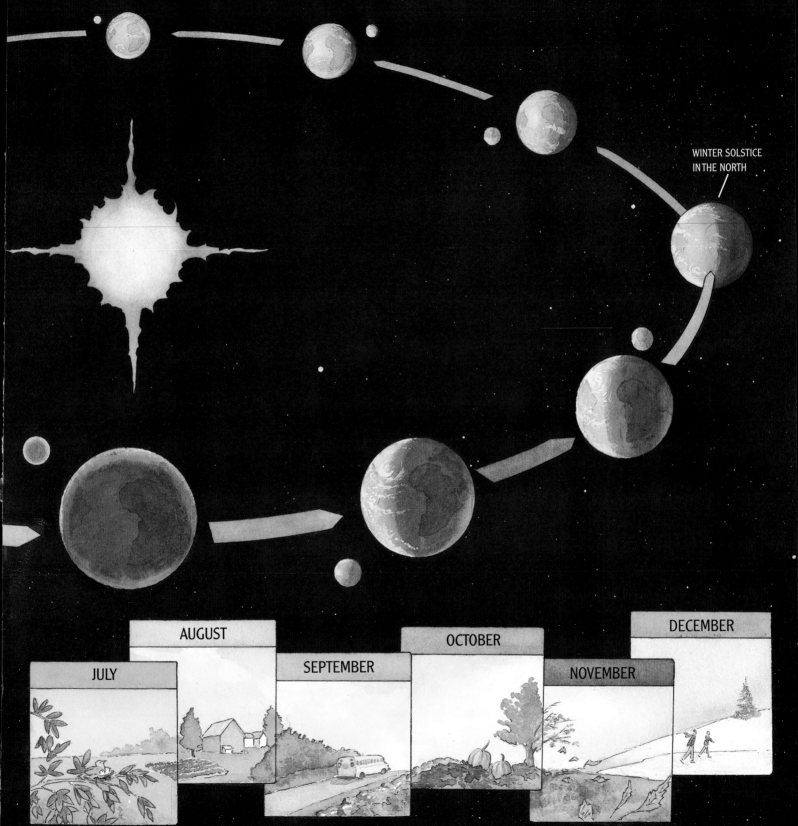

WINTER SOLSTICE
IN THE NORTH

JULY

AUGUST

SEPTEMBER

OCTOBER

NOVEMBER

DECEMBER

The Earth is round like a ball and
it moves in circular motions.
It changes in patterns, called cycles,
that go round and round
like the wheels on a bike.

## ABOUT THE AUTHOR AND ARTIST

Michael Elsohn Ross lives at the entrance of Yosemite National Park, California, on a bluff overlooking the wild Merced river. Both his wife and teenage daughter are published poets and avid outdoors people. For more than twenty-five years Michael has been teaching visitors to Yosemite about the plants, animals, and geology of the park. He leads classes and backpack trips for the Yosemite Association and is the educational director of Yosemite Guides. His work in the park and as a science educator have inspired him to write more than thirty books for young people.

Growing up in rural Maine, Gustav Moore's boyhood adventures in the woods and fields of his family's farm have given him a deep appreciation and love of the natural world. His colorful and detailed watercolor paintings reflect this beauty and wonder of nature. Gustav works and lives in Maine, where he still wanders the open pastures of the family farm, finding inspiration in the cycles of nature.